T0065599

Tales of a
Christian Coonhunter

William T. Stackhouse

WESTBOW
P R E S S®
A DIVISION OF THOMAS NELSON
& ZONDERVAN

Scripture quotations are from The Holy Bible, English Standard Version®
(ESV®), copyright © 2001 by Crossway, a publishing ministry of
Good News Publishers. Used by permission. All rights reserved.

WestBow Press books may be ordered through booksellers or by contacting:

WestBow Press
A Division of Thomas Nelson & Zondervan
1663 Liberty Drive
Bloomington, IN 47403
www.westbowpress.com
1 (866) 928-1240

ISBN: 978-1-5127-4736-2 (sc)
ISBN: 978-1-5127-4737-9 (e)

Print information available on the last page.

WestBow Press rev. date: 6/30/2016

Contents

I would like to thank God for giving me the opportunity to write this book; my wife, Sarah, for all that she does; my mother, Sally, who introduced me to God; my brother and his wife, Lytle and Casey, for all that they do; Tom Gray for selling me my bluetick, Chief; Joe and Geraldine Day for helping to teach me Biblical values, Through Kat's Eye Photography for capturing the photos used for the cover photo and author photo, and thank you to the staff at Westbow Press for publishing my book. May God bless you all.

John 3:16 "For God so loved the world that he gave his only Son, that whoever believes in him should not perish but have eternal life."

Genesis 27:3 "Now then, take your weapons, your quiver and your bow, and go out to the field and hunt game for me."

Introduction

This book was written with the pleasure hunter in mind and some aspects of the competition world as well, but mainly it focuses on the enjoyment of owning and hunting the pleasure coonhound, and who gave us this great way of life, GOD. As you read, you will find tips on training different types of dogs and breeds as well as all kinds of hunting methods while pleasure hunting in the woods. It takes an interesting view on medicating your dog and housing your dog as well as what type of food your dog might need. I have over 25 years of experience hunting, training and caring for all breeds of coon hounds. I also used to be employed at a nationally known English bird dog kennel where I was caretaker of sixty various dogs from the small Jack Russell Terrier to the large German Shepard and over thirty English Bird dogs all at the same time.

I hope you enjoy reading this book and take away in your mind some memories of your own, as well as some helpful tips on what dog is right for you, as well as a whole new outlook on coon hounds and the way they can be used. Also try to keep in mind that I usually speak my mind on matters and that I usually find myself politically incorrect. This is because of my belief in living by God's word, excepting Jesus Christ as my Lord and Savior and letting the Holy Spirit be my guide to light the way. I give all praises, power and glory to God Almighty and

I pray that those who read this book will hopefully understand that all things should be done for the Glory of God and I also pray that this book may help plant a seed for God and may your seed grow in faith through our Lord, God.

So sit back, turn off the tube and let your mind at ease as you read about this wonderful pastime that God has blessed us with that we call coonhunting.

CHAPTER 1

Hooked

I believe I was around four years old the first time that I remember being in the woods at night hunting coon. My mom says I was younger than that but it was around then when I first remember it myself. The dog was a Hammer bred Bluetick that my dad bought from the Northern Blue Kennels of Dave Dean. For a boy of only four years old, the dog was a mighty big hound. He had a nice mouth and was a very nice looking hound. As a remember it, my twin brother and I woke up to the hounds treeing in some hardwoods down over the bank. We got out of the truck and stood in the road with Dad and his two hunting buddies. We all went down the bank into the stateland. When we got to the tree, the two Walkers and the Bluetick were treeing pretty hard. It was also pretty cold that night and I can remember it like it was yesterday. By the time we got back to the truck, my brother and I were complaining that our feet were hurting because they were so cold. Our boots were rubber black barn boots with a red stripe going around the tops. Once we got back in the truck and got the heat on our feet, we, of course, wanted to keep going. But Dad said, as Dad usually did, "It's late. We will call it a night and end it on a good note." Who knew how many drops were made that night. My brother and I used to be put to sleep by driving around the stateland late at night when we were kids, just enjoying the ride. Coonhunting was done by road hunting, and we were probably out for a few hours being watched by my mom while the first drops were being done. Regardless, my brother and I were hooked for life.

CHAPTER 2

Sarge

Sarge was the first coondog that I remember that belonged to my brother and me. Plus, he was a broke coon dog. Dad worked for the county highway department and he had a really good friend that worked there as well. In the early 90's, his friend had a Nite Champion dog that he called Lady. Lady was the best registered dog that I have ever been in the woods with. Well his friend took Sarge and Lady hunting one night and old Sarge started fighting with Lady on the tree. Now, the owner wouldn't put up with that and I don't blame him. He also knew of two twin boys that would hunt Sarge by himself. So Lytle and I were real excited when Dad told us we were getting a broke coondog. The first time I remember Sarge running track, it was in the fall of the year. We went up in the state land and pulled over on the side of the road with Dad's old 1988 Ford F-150. On the right hand side of the road were about five or ten apple trees. We let old Sarge go in the woods and we sat on the tailgate and waited for some action. It was a clear night, a little chilly, and you could see the bright moon and stars against the big black sky. Then all of a sudden we heard Sarge open up with a few chops. I remember the big smile on my face and the excited fascination I felt wondering just what he was doing and how awesome it felt to hear the hound open up for the first time. I asked Dad what he was doing and he explained to me that Sarge was running a coon track. Then a few minutes later he wouldn't stop barking and he wasn't moving anymore either. Dad said, "Well boys lets go see what he's got." I was a young boy, of a little more than twelve years old, and there was no music in the world that could compare with the sound of that hound treeing that coon.

Well, we got up to the tree and Sarge was treeing really hard on an apple tree. But the only problem was that Sarge was about eight feet in the tree and the coon wasn't far from him. Dad was totally against climbing a tree, but it wasn't too high, so between my Brother and I, we got Sarge down out of the tree. Sarge was a grade coonhound with reddish ears and a mostly white body. If I had to guess, I would say he was a little muscled up, 60-pound Walker dog. We were some happy to have him. Now my Dad developed rheumatoid arthritis but still tried to work, but after the guys at work had to help him out of his truck, he finally had to go see the Doctor. and started taking medicine for his crippling arthritis. He didn't let it take his life until he was 61 years of age. Daddy was diagnosed with the arthritis at 35 years old. Through the pain he worked and hunted until he was about 55. Because of Dad's handicapped state, we hunted Sarge in a lot of cornfields trying to hit hot tracks.

We let Sarge go in the neighbor's cornfield and old Sarge opened up. The hair stood up on my neck with excitement. Being a hot track, it didn't take Sarge long to track that coon. Now, Dad had to buy a .22 rifle, because our cabin that we lived in caught fire and burnt up all of Dad's guns. That night would be the first coon I ever shot out of a tree. The gun had a mahogany colored wooden stock with a gold colored trigger. I stood in the corn field and shot the coon out of the tall maple tree that was in a hedgerow of trees. It was another cool crisp night where old Sarge looked like a million bucks to a starry eyed young boy who was totally into coonhunting. I couldn't stop thinking of coonhunting with my dog.

The doctor had my Dad try to walk as much as he could, so I went walking with Dad a lot. We tried to make it a mile and sometimes I had to drive the truck so Dad could lean on it because of his illness. We took Sarge along and one day we let him go. He went out ahead of us hunting. Now Sarge had a hot nose and he hunted really close. That made him perfect for our situation. All of a sudden, Sarge struck a track. I had never run a coon in the day time before. In no time he sounded like he was treed, but his voice sounded muffled. When we got up to him it was quite obvious why he sounded muffled. Sarge had ran the track right into a culvert in the road. He had the coon bayed in the culvert and was too big to fit in there to chase him out the other side of the road. This taught me two new things about hunting coon. First of all, coon really do travel in the daytime, sometimes. Second, that you are not always going to tree your coon in a tree.

The second time we had Sarge tree in the daytime, was on another walk with Dad. It was only about six hundred yards from where we treed the other coon in the culvert. It was on a different day and if I remember right it was a few months later. This time, he ended up treeing the coon in a really, really tall hemlock. It can be tough or impossible to find the coon in a hemlock tree.

In the fall of the year the leaves were off and the ground was a blanket of reds, yellows and browns among the maple trees.

It was a full moon out, clear sky and the night air coming in and going out of our mouths in the moon light looked as cold as the ice in the mud puddles on the dirt road. It was a perfect night to run coon. Although, Dad had always told us that we were in for an unusual night because of the full moon. This was because on a bright night we tend to run coon that would run a long way or it can be real enticing for young hounds to run deer if they weren't already broke off of them.

Dad was right as always. On this hunt we had three of my older cousins along and my uncle. We took Sarge up real deep in the state land and dropped him off in one of the spots that had some apple trees in it. Sarge was a little tight mouthed until he got the track warmed up. He ran the track a good mile to the south, crisscrossing and lopping all the way. He then brought the track back up beyond us. We drove the truck up to him and not very far off the road was Sarge treed in a huge pine tree. The coon climbed almost all the way to the top, but would stay on the other side of the tree, only looking occasionally to tease us. This is where the unusual part comes in and it was even scary. I'll start by saying this: Dad sometimes carried a shotgun with birdshot behind the seat of his old Ford to make a coon look if they weren't showing those amber eyes. Then, we noticed that one of my cousins was about half way up the tree (which we didn't encourage) and we were all concentrating on him and the coon. While Dad and I and all the others were concentrating on that, all of a sudden, we heard a huge thunderous bang!!! Flames shot out of the gun a foot and a half long. All I could hear was the ringing in my ear and the birdshot flying through the air and hitting the limbs of the pine tree. One of my other cousins, unnoticed to any of us, snuck into Dad's truck, grabbed the Ithaca single shot, threw in some birdshot from the glove compartment and scared the living day lights out of everyone involved. My cousin in the tree had words come out of his mouth that I don't think the Jerry Springer show has ever heard. Everyone started yelling at my cousin with the gun and he just said in the only way that he could, "I just wanted to make him look."

Thank God nobody got hurt. Sarge kept treeing and that memory is one I will never forget. Now when my brother and I reminisce about the old times growing up, that story always surfaces. All we can do is laugh at it because it was so bizarre and Dad would crack jokes about it and make us laugh. Nevertheless, we did stop hunting with our cousin (the one with the gun.) It taught me to make sure you know where everyone is that is hunting with you and especially take extra caution around the tree. It would be a shame to have someone get hurt or killed over a ringtail.

My advice to anyone who is looking to tree quick coon for medical reasons, school the next day, work, or your taking a youngster out for the first couple of times: keep it easy. Hit cornfields when the corn is in the milk or apple orchards when the coon is in the apples. We even hit a dumpster now and then at a campsite that is busy during the week but not on the weekends. Just remember, if the dog is too slow for competition hunting, there is always an old timer that would enjoy a slower dog to keep up with. Or a dog that fights on tree is still useful to a youngster that just wants to enjoy listening to a single dog run coon and get the blood boiling or the hair stand up on the back of their neck. As long as the dog isn't ill or mean towards people in any way, then the dog can still make some memories with him or her. I don't advise breeding to a mean dog, but that is for another story and chapter.

CHAPTER 3

Plott and Trapper

Plott and Trapper were a one-two punch on raccoon and a real deal team at treeing summer time coon. I say summer time coon, because Plott would run deer in the snow. She was a grade Plott hound, but hands down, the best grade dog that I ever had the privilege of walking behind in the woods to the date of this books writings. As long as there was no snow on the ground, because then she would have a deer bayed on the snow. Spring, Summer and Fall she would flat out make your jaw drop as to how good of a track dog she was and she also had that sit-down-tree-dog style that has been bred out of so many hounds of today. I believe she had more of a hot nose and this was also part of what made her so accurate. I have seen her work a cold trail that ended with a coon in the tree also.

It is my opinion that Trapper was Plott's sidekick. Yes, he could tree his own coon but four out of five trees, that little female Plott dog would smoke the track ahead of Trapper, the Treeing Walker. When it came to road hunting, Old Plott would be in front of all the hounds in the pack. In fact, Trapper was the only dog around that could keep up with Plott, but even he was about four car lengths behind her. I'm talking an

80's station wagon car length. We used to follow those two hounds with my Dad driving his 1988 Ford F-150 and my cousin, who owned the two dogs, driving his 1960's Chevy pick-up. The one important trait that Trapper had over Plott was the fact that he would not run a deer, even if the deer was ten feet in front of him. No sirree, he would come back to us with his tail between his legs and then we knew what the story was. He was a great check dog.

On some nights we would just turn those two hounds loose at the coop and let them go. They would either head straight behind the house, through the pasture and strike a track somewhere in the pasture or in the stateland up the road. They also would go down to the old beaver pond and run the coon up the hill through the hay field or cornfield and into the hardwoods. I remember Plott treeing a coon between the beaver pond and the field on a little sapling that was only about fifteen feet tall. She was hot on the trail when her and old Trapper pulled up and treed with the rain coming down. The coon was bending the tree because the trunk of the tree wasn't very big around.

The older standard trucks used to come with a granny first gear. You could put your truck in first and let the clutch out, then just idle behind the dog and enjoy watching the dog work the road with their noses drifting and searching this way and that. But with Old Plott, no way buddy! Dad clocked her on most nights flat out running at 35 miles per hour and she was hunting. Going that fast and striking track from the road was her specialty. A lot of hounds would work the road and go off investigating curiously. Plott would change course and leap from center road to bank in one fast move and strike track in midair. Now don't get me wrong she had her faults

and she wasn't perfect, but she was awesome at doing what she did. After she struck track, whether you were road hunting, hardwood hunting in dry leaves or dropping her in a corn field, I would say ninety or ninety-five percent of the time you would find Plott and Trapper pulled up under the tree with Trapper and his two front feet on the wood and the little Plott sitting on her rear chopping away at the coon. Plott was her name and she was a grade Plott hound. Trapper was a Treeing Walker. Even still Dad, my brother and myself wanted to breed those two hounds together. Because we were pleasure hunters, papers at that time didn't matter to us. Unfortunately, Plott only came in heat one time in her life and we missed our chance to find out what could have been. I guess that is proof of how much she loved to hunt. It was almost like she didn't have or want to take the time to have a litter of pups. All she wanted to do was hunt. That is my only regret with those two hounds, is that we never got any pups out of them. I was with her and my cousin on her last tree. She was older now and getting on in years. The coon was finally too fast and the den tree was empty. It was about eight feet tall and we could see all the way to the top from inside the tree. She ended looking like a frosty mouth Plott. Then she died of old age in her coop that winter. Some dogs are big and some dogs are small, but there will never be a dog with more heart come fall.

Now-a-days, I have a shock collar for dogs that want to bump a deer, but back then nobody could seem to come up with the money or means to get one. They work great in the hands of someone who knows how to use one. I often wonder just how good the little Plott female could have been if she had been broken off of the deer. Because, then we could have hunted her when the snow was on also! I talked with Dave

Dean a while back and we had a good talk about E-collars and their uses. Dave is old school and a nice guy with a ton of hound information. Long story short, sometimes the E-collar can do more damage than good on some hounds if the operator doesn't understand starting out on the low setting and gradually increasing the intensity, if necessary. These were wise words from Dave that has benefited me to this very day. Thank you Dave, your friend Bill Stackhouse.

CHAPTER 4

Random Experiences = Knowledge

If you hear of a broke coondog that lost a hind leg or the use of it, don't pass it up if that is all that is wrong with the dog. If the dog has the heart, the dog may be a little slower, but could still enjoy many years of hunting and you could, too. Susie was a Bluetick that helped tree a lot of coon for us and other dogs. Certain three legged dogs can make good pup trainers at an earlier age than normal and still be a dog of great value to you and your pack of hounds. This is because with only three legs they are slower and easy for the pups to keep up with. If you have a dog that has more skin or tender skin around the neck you can keep them in a chain link kennel without a collar on for their protection. I had an English Bluetick once that was very sensitive to collars and moisture. This is why I prefer straw over hay as bedding because hay traps and holds moisture in as where straw stays dryer and is more comfortable for your hound. It shouldn't give your dog any problems. But hay works great for dogs that are not sensitive. If this doesn't work, you can also use a horse blanket, as long as it stays dry. I currently have a Walker who is now on chain for hunting, but when she was on the bench show circuit, I kept her in the chain link kennel so the chain didn't leave a gray stain on her white chest.

I like a hound that has a big bawl mouth, long ears, great conformation and great color of any kind. But I would pass on all of those traits if that dog wouldn't hunt and the dog at the next coop was a squeaky, chop mouth, short eared, flat footed swayback with colors of a retriever if that dog could get the job done in the woods. I would take the one less desirable to look at and hear. I guess what I am trying to say is, don't pass on ability for looks if you want a coondog that lives up to the name of coondog. I once knew of a dog that would tip her water bucket over within a few minutes after she would get her water and food. This was a strong genetic dislike. I say genetic because all of her pups by around four months old would do the same exact thing and she was bred to many different males of different breeds. The other trait that we noticed was, most of her litters that she threw would be man-aggressive by ten or eleven months old, but she was not. Whenever you see a trait in a dog that is undesirable to the point that you cannot tolerate that trait, my advice is to not make him or her breeding stock.

I went hunting with one of my friends who had a Black and Tan/Bloodhound cross and a Redbone/Bloodhound cross. They were both making their way up a leaning tree that went probably twenty-five to thirty feet in the air. With both hounds treeing hard, the red dog slowly started down the tree with us calling him down. Then we began to try to help by calling the Black and Tan cross and at about ten feet he slipped and fell. A little rattled, he then jumped up and right back up the leaning tree he went. Then the unfortunate thing happened. He began treeing so hard that he lost his balance and fell to the ground again. The dog let out a yelp and got up with a limp.

He was not physically hurt bad, but the mental side of treeing was ruined. I told my friend that I feared the hound would not tree again if he related the pain with treeing. My friend was concerned and he said, "Time will tell, I guess." Sometimes, it seems like more than not, I would like to be wrong about a feeling especially if it is about something negative like that. As time would tell my friend said he took the dog hunting several times after that and the dog would not tree or hang around the tree. He would simply run track, mill around the tree a little, then move on to find another track. Years later, this taught me two things. One, the dog was a good tree dog that got messed up naturally. Second, by all means, try not to let anything negative happen around the tree, especially to young hounds, like fights or anything of this nature to a hound.

My thoughts on some competition events are this: field trials are fine and fun, but not if the field trial starts at 2:00pm and a couple of the other hounds have been ran on the course a couple hours before for an advantage over the other hounds. I went to a field trial once with a hound that was as accurate and fast as they come. We got beat from the above scenario by a hound that knew the course so well he skipped part of the trail, never put his nose to the ground or the air and ran straight to the tree. My dog got second and almost got tree before Ole Straight Arrow let out his first bark. The only way to solve this in an easy fashion is pure old fashion honesty by all competitors. I was told by the other owner/handler that his dog only lacked five points from being a field champion and that was all he cared about getting. Now that's not the type of honesty I was talking about. If you go for the fun of it, you will have a lot better time. Also, ask them to run the trail from the field to the tree like a real coon would, not the other way around.

CHAPTER 5

Misty

Misty was a UKC registered Black and Tan coonhound. My dad got this hound as a young dog and worked with her a lot. Dad worked with this hound until she was two years old. She was a beautiful dog, but Dad finally grew tired of getting no progress out of the dog so he sold her to my cousin. He kept working with her until she was a finished coonhound.

Then finally at the age of two and a half, she started to tree coon. This is a good example of some dogs just maturing later in life than others. If you have hunted a dog for 2 ½ years and still, you are not treeing coon and the dog has had proper exposure to the correct environment of training, then you have a hound that might be good for something else, but not for treeing coon. However, I personally don't wait any longer than two years. If they don't start by sixteen months, then I don't consider them for my breeding program. My hounds usually get started at 10 months. A lot will start at four months old but I will not let or expose them to caged coon until later.

I like to start my hounds no sooner than ten months, but they need to be mentally mature enough to start that early. Misty was what I called a grand pleasure style coon dog. We would walk her out in the woods and she would go out ahead of us and we would sit on a log or an old tree. Then we would listen to see if she would open up and start running a track. Sometimes you would have to walk her quite some ways to get her on a track and, to me, that was part of the fun in the hunt, getting to watch her work and seeing the track get warmed up. Then she was off and I would say that she wasn't a slow track dog at all.

One night my cousin, my brother and I went hunting in a bunch of maple trees with hayfields and apple trees spread out through them. Misty struck a track with a few chops, and away we went. Boy she was really working that track and moving it pretty darn fast, slashing this way and that. We sat on the edge of the cut-out road that ran up to the hayfields and listened. She was all the way up on top of the ridge when she tapped and moved on with the track. She was quiet for just a few moments and ran the track around the beaver pond. Then, BANG! She started chopping her head off. We knew then that she had "old mister ringtail" up a tree. The only problem was it would have taken a D-8 Cat Dozer to get through the buck brush and over the next ridge to get to her. So we went back to the truck and drove around the hill to her. Sure enough she had the coon and did a really good job at getting the right tree.

This showed us just how tough of a coon track she could really handle if the conditions were right. We hunted her in cornfields, hardwoods and swamps but she did do something that I noticed to be very strange to me at the time. She was very smart. Misty started to run less and less open on track. In fact, the older she got, the more to being a silent dog she got to be. She might have started slow, but she got a lot more intelligent the older she got and the more track experience she got. Somehow it occurred to her that if she was quiet on track, she could get them treed faster. Now that is a smart dog! But the downfall to it was that I missed hearing her beautiful voice on track. She was a real pleasure to hunt and follow in the woods.

I do wish I could find her bloodline again, but I am afraid it has been long gone. I have tried to find out what type of breeding she had in her, but to no success, unfortunately. I will always remember the hound that started late, but finished GREAT! She was a very nice Black and Tan coondog indeed.

CHAPTER 6

Dog Houses and Food

The simple truth about dogfood is to buy a top quality dog food that will keep your dog healthy and looking and feeling great. On the off season I personally feed a dogfood that is 21% crude protein minimum. The crude fat minimum is 10%. This is fed in the summer to my hounds when they don't need a lot of energy from the protein. The fat percentage is also lower because they don't need to put on extra fat because they are not as active and not dealing with cold weather. I also must say that you should always have a fresh supply of water for your hounds. When my hounds are being hunted a lot or are in competition, I like to bump them up to a higher quality dogfood that has 27% crude protein and a fat content of 15%. This also applies for my dogs in the winter months. It really helps when the temperatures are around 0 degrees. I am not a veterinarian, but this is what works for me. However, I don't recommend feeding a protein too high or a fat content too high, either. I have not ever had a hound that was too fat, but common sense goes along way. My brother fed a black and tan dog food that was 32% protein. After three days she was peeing blood. We talked about it and he stopped feeding such high protein. Immediately in a day and a half she was back to normal and not peeing any more blood. This also happened to a Walker female and a Bluetick/Plott cross female that our friend had owned. I am not saying this will happen to every dog, but in my experiences I would pass on too high of protein with those kinds of results. If you feed house scraps or the most expensive dog food on the planet, always, always, always remember to have fresh water for your hound available at all times. I personally water my dogs two and sometimes three times a day when the weather is real hot in the summer. I should add that meat based dog food is the best food, however I have made a bench show champion out of feeding nothing but 15% fat, 27% protein, corn based dogfood with some table scraps mixed in about once a week. I would also like to add that in the winter I mix warm water with the dogfood just enough to cover the food. This will ensure that your dog will not get dehydrated in the cold winter months. Plus, the warm water will help warm them up. After they are used to it they will look forward to the hot meal. You might like it too, because it cuts down on buckets you carry in the deep snow and you only have to use one big old cooking pot to feed the dogs with instead of two for each hound. They still need fresh water in the winter.

I also feel that I should touch on the debate of whether or not you should give your dogs table scraps. Well, I have personally fed all of my hounds table scraps since I was five years old. As I sit here at my table, at the time of this writing, I see left over pieces of hot dogs, baked beans, macaroni salad, wheat thins and wheat bread. This is all leftover from my kids. I would not hesitate for a second to mix this in with a scoop of dog food. Before there was the invention of dogfood, how do people think the old timers fed their hounds? It was table scrapes or raw meat from the butcher or game that had been harvested.

A clean, warm and dry doghouse is a must for my dog. I personally built a doghouse that is in a triangle slope, with shingles on the outside. You can put tarpaper between the shingles and the boards or the plywood, whatever ones you use. This works as an insulation for the dogs. It is simple and efficient. In the winter it keeps the heat in. It also keeps the dogs cool in the summer. I put about one foot of straw in the doghouse for bedding and this works very well for all year long. When it is real hot out and my dogs are under the maple trees for shade, they will still go inside the dog house for comfort because of the way they are built, even with being surrounded by shade trees. I also put the doghouse on top of a pallet. I simply nail the bottom of the doghouse to the top of the pallet. Now with the pallet on the ground and the doghouse off of the ground, it creates a ventilation draft under the doghouse and through the pallet for dry floorboards. This will make the dog happy and it will make you happy because the doghouse will last a lot longer. Also, always make sure your dog has shade. Remember, God made us the caretakers of the animals.

CHAPTER 7

Bell the Black & Tan

Ole Bell was a forty-pound little Black and Tan that was a kind hearted dog to people and animals. But not the varmints that she hunted. My brother had her given to him by a friend that was not able to hunt her anymore and he knew that we would hunt the dog and not just keep her on the chain at the coop. She was a purebred Black and Tan, but her papers got lost when she was a puppy. She was given to us as a broke hound. But she didn't just run coon. My brother liked to just run her on coon and I used her on coon and opossum. Unfortunately, she would also tree porcupine, which was fine, but not when she got into a tussle with one. We really didn't have too much of a problem with her catching up with a porcupine because she was a real slow track dog. She would straddle a track and sometimes walk, sometimes halfway jog, but never run and she would smoke the track like it was red hot.

She also had a cold nose and when you combine a cold nose with a slow track dog, a lot of times you were in for a long night if you hunted Bell in the hard woods in thin coon country. The other thing that was a blessing for an older pleasure hunter or a major fault for a competition hunter was the fact that you had to walk Bell when you took her hunting. She would go out about fifty-hundred yards, circle and come back. This may have been from her breeding, but I really think that with this particular hound it was the way she was trained. You see, her previous owner basically just walked her around cornfields and when she was about two years old, she all of a sudden started treeing coon. This was good, but it got her used to hunting with someone and not for someone. But again, her breeding also played a big part in how she hunted.

Now, I have been in some competitions with dogs that have champion status success, so I can appreciate the competition hound and all the hard work it takes the dog and handler to achieve this degree. However, there are still places in this world for dogs like Ole Bell, that wasn't a great coondog, but could get the job done. A dog like this works great if you can't get around quite as good as you used to. Or if you want to take a youngster to the woods and get them interested in coon hunting. She was open on track with a chop mouth. Then when she treed, it turned into a steady chop. I used to take her to cornfields or other places that I figured I could get her on a hot coon track, so it didn't take too long to tree, but yet, a good half hour to forty minutes would produce a treed coon or opossum and a great big huge grin on my face. Mainly because I knew she had fun, I had fun and I knew that not just anyone would keep a dog that had Bell's hunting style. She was real accurate and I believe that was because of the fact that she put her nose to the ground and tracked the varmints instead of just winding. Some dogs are real accurate on winding lay-up coon, and that also can make a dog a real fast dog on track because they are running to catch, but ole Bell ran the track to track first, then to tree.

I like both styles of trailing, as long as the dog is accurate and has the coon in the tree when I get there. I currently own a Treeing Walker female that I made into a bench show Champion this past summer. Now she puts her nose to the ground and drifts the track when necessary, but she is always running and is very accurate. She is a real fast track dog and combines both tracking styles. When we had Bell, the Black and Tan dog papers were not on our minds as much so we crossed her with a male Treeing Walker that my brother had at the time with not much success. Bell brought accuracy and treeing power to the table. The Walker brought the speed on track to the table. So we figured we would try to combine the two to try to bring out the best of both worlds in the pups, but it didn't work. The genes just were not meant to be for the pup that we kept. The other pups I can't speak for though. I can only remember where three of the six went. One we kept and the other two ended up acting like guard dogs because they were more house pets than anything and didn't really get a fair shake in the woods.

The one that we kept would run track, but just never came into treeing. I think he could have been a good dog for game that left tracks but didn't tree. For example, red fox or snowshoe rabbit or maybe even coyotes because he was a fairly quick track dog. He got his speed on track from his father and his nose power from his mother. His father wasn't a great tree dog for us and, unfortunately, he inherited that trait as well.

One day, my wife and I were driving our UTV up in the woods when, right in the daytime a coon crossed the road right in front of us. I thought about it and then we went straight down to my brother's house to pick up Bell. It was still daylight and would be for about an hour and a half more. My brother and I brought up Bell and let her go where I saw the coon cross the road. She started to wag her tail, took a few steps down into the pines and opened up. The chase was on! We headed down after her. Even though Ole Bell was a slow track dog, she didn't miss much at all. She worked the track down over a bank and through the tall pine trees. The forest floor was covered with red pine needles that were dead and had fell the year before. This did make for real dry and tough tracking conditions, but with her nose and the freshly laid track, she ended up working it down to the beaver pond and across the top of the beaver dam. She then located with a short bawl and had the coon. We could see the coon from the hill. We had to go down to get to her. It was very fascinating to watch her use her nose and to see her tail wag even faster as the track warmed up. She took a while to tree it but that was okay. In my book it was sweet music to listen to and I learned something: ALWAYS TAKE YOUR COMPASS!

We had hunted those woods all our lives. It was daylight and we were in a hurry to go hunting. I have been lost before and said "I will never go to the woods without my compass." But, I slipped up and forgot it and paid for it, almost. After Bell treed, there was a disagreement with my brother about which way the road was. A long story short, we got back to the road and it was just before pitch dark. It taught me that even in timber that you have been in all your life, hunting coon, deer and turkey you can still get confused when the adrenaline is pumping and you're in a hurry.

Always take a compass and/or a GPS. I have found that both, or at least two compasses should be efficient. I got in the habit of carrying a compass that north, south, east and west all glow in the dark. The arrows also glow in the dark. Also, carry a backup flashlight. I once was in the woods at night, my dog treed and the only light I had, had blown the only bulb I had. I thank God I had a glow in the dark compass so I could find my way out of the woods. A few branches to the face and tripping over a few dead trees reminded me to be more prepared.

CHAPTER 8

Hard Lessons About The Right Ingredients

I went looking for a coondog to buy and I heard that this man had a lot of good coondogs that I could buy if I wanted. Well, I went to his house and talked with the man. He told me he had some hounds and wanted to know what I was looking for. I said," I am looking for a dog I could start this fall." He said," I just had a litter of pups that would be ready around that time and they are out of really good old time bloodlines that you cannot find anymore." So, we went out to the dogs and saw them. These pups had nice long ears, deep rich color and already deep bawl mouths. They looked like a picture of the perfect litter of pups. The parents were very houndy looking as well. So, I bought one. This was the beginning of a hard lesson about the ingredients of a real coondog.

Over the years, I had hunted with coonhounds that were purebred dogs, as well as mixed bred dogs that were one hundred percent coonhound with mixed ancestry in different breeds. I experienced good hounds and bad or worthless hounds for hunting in both categories.

These hounds that this man had were mixed with a type of hound that isn't bred for treeing. I ended up unhappy with the outcome of several dogs from different litters. The hounds I had bought from him would run track openly but never would settle in on treeing even a little bit. Out of about twenty hounds that were crossed with coonhounds and this other type of hound, only two of these dogs would actually tree a coon. The first of the two dogs was dead silent and extremely inaccurate. The second dog would trail and tree but needed the first dog to help keep it straight. Over a period of about five years, I did some experimenting with these hounds. I noticed that most of them would trail and tree in the daylight on coon, Farrell cats and scent drags. But at night when they couldn't see their quarry, they would just simply shut down at the tree and wouldn't tree. On trail they couldn't see the game that they pursued. Some were open, but the outcome had ended up not treeing when they found the tree at night. So, they would tree if they could see the game and they were also open on track.

My experience in this experiment, as well as over thirty years of hunting coonhounds and other types of hounds, has taught me a couple of things about the ingredients of tree dogs. For one, just because a dog will tree in the daytime doesn't mean that they will tree at night when they cannot see the game. Also, when you are looking to tree coon at night, my advice to anyone is to find out about the dog's true ancestry as far back as you want to, at least for three generations. I would advise you to make sure that all ancestors on both sides of the sire and dam were legitimate coondogs that would tree a coon. Don't get me wrong, I am not saying all of the pups produced have to be, but all the dogs in a three generation that are up close to the pups you are buying should have a high percentage of good coonhounds involved in the bloodlines.

This also brings me to a few points I want to touch on that involves dog papers, breeding dogs and money involved. Dog papers or a pedigree can be a very useful tool in the hands of the right person. The titles and accomplishments of the dog's ancestry help play a part in the purchase of your next pup and I, personally, use this tool to my advantage whenever possible. But I should add something that Dad taught me many years ago and it still stands true to this day. Papers don't make coondogs! Yes, they do give you a clear picture of what you are dealing with in the genetic make-up of your pup prospect, if, like I said before, the hands of the person holding the papers are honest and didn't just put the papers on the dog to make a sale!

As far as money goes, it is up to you to determine how much and how deep you want to go into this sport. I, personally, don't like to spend a lot of money on purchasing hounds. I have bought dogs out of World Champion bloodlines with better results out of my pet beagle, who was running loose at one time and had treed a coon. I have also paid a good price for a pup with good bloodlines and had great results. I once traveled four hours away to see a dog run and had the opportunity to buy the dog if I wanted to. Well, the dog did tree one hot coon and it never treed another one for me. That taught me two lessons. One: if you try out a dog, make sure you see it tree more than one coon. And second: make sure you see the dog run with company because the last thing you want to do is waste your money on a tree fighter. My brother went all the way out to Indiana from central New York to breed his female to a who's-who of treeing Walker stud dogs.

He ended up with no pups. The man was very nice about it and only wanted a pup for the service if she had any. But it did cost my brother a lot in gas, food and a hotel room. So it is all up to you and remember, if you don't mind mix-bred hounds and just love to pleasure hunt, then maybe a mix-bred dog of proven ancestry is the ticket for you. These types of dogs are usually cheaper. Sometimes a kennel breeder will have more than one breed of coonhounds and one gets loose and breeds another dog of different breed type. Sometimes they sell the pups at a quarter of the cost of a purebred because the pups are mixed and without papers. But, like I have said before, the papers don't make the coondogs; it is in the genetic make-up of what God put in them. I have also found that some dogs that don't make coondogs because they don't tree, can make really good coyote hounds or other types of dogs if they don't have the treeing instinct in them.

No matter how well our hounds are bred or whether or not they have pedigree papers, the simple but hard fact is, that some hounds just need to be culled. If you have a coondog that attacked other animals, people or just cannot wait to sink its teeth into something, you have a perfect candidate to be culled. You cannot use this type of dog for hunting because it is too quarrelsome and you cannot use it for a house dog. It cannot be trusted! You would be doing the dog, the people involved, other animals and especially innocent little children a favor by putting an animal like that to sleep permanently. Remember, even guard dogs should not bite the hand that feeds them. Because dogs have intelligence and they do what they are bred for. A coondog is no different in the sense that they should also do what they are bred for naturally.

CHAPTER 9

Jade

I told one of my hunting friends that I was in the market for a coondog that would run and tree a coon. He called me up and told me that there was an ad in the Bloodlines magazine and he gave me the phone number. It was a Treeing Walker that was about two years old. Well, I talked to the man on the phone and made arrangements to go out and see her. He wanted four hundred dollars for her and he lived four hours away. I, for one, do not like to travel, but we are talking about a started Walker with papers that was of the who's who of the Treeing Walker breed.

Well, my brother and I rented 2 motel rooms, one for my wife and myself and one for him and his wife. I told my brother that I had to see a coon in the tree before I would buy the dog. At the first drop we let her go in a cornfield and she opened real strong. She worked the track for about twenty-five minutes. But I also noticed that the more she was out there, the less she used her mouth to the point where she didn't say anything. Well my brother said "what do you think?" I replied, "I need to see more." Now he was going to buy half of her, so he also had to be happy with her also. On the second drop, it was another cornfield and the same thing happened again, almost exactly the same way as before. She opened well, but the longer the track went, the less she opened and eventually she would say nothing. Now she was 0-2 on two cornfield coontracks that should have been easily treed. The owner told us that he wanted to go get her alone, because she was so far out there. As he was gone, my brother and I took the time to discuss the dog and he wanted to know what I thought about her. I told him I don't like her and that I was pretty sure that she was running track backwards. We had some words like brothers do and he said he didn't come this far to not bring something home. So I had to agree because he was paying for half the dog and trip. We waited for a long time for him to get back and when he did, Jade was with him. So for the third time, we made a drop, but this time we made a drop down a walking trail where it was controlled by the state. The man who owned Jade told us that this is where the Indians used to salt the fish, so they would keep longer and he showed us the real deep hole of water where the natural salt and water were used. That was really neat!

We walked down the groomed trail and Jade automatically started treeing. She ran no track and just slammed a cherry tree with a coon in it. I have to admit that I did say I would buy her if I saw a coon and it did look impressive. So we bought the hound. I did notice that this man had a cell phone and this was about the time when people started having them a lot. His brother called him and wanted to know how the showing was going. He told his brother that Jade treed a coon. As we got back home, I started putting two and two together. I realized that I was pretty sure he pulled the wool over our eyes on that hound. First of all, I was in my early twenties, but I knew a track dog when I saw one. And the first red flag was when I heard Jade run the track backward twice. The second red flag was when it took Jade's owner forty-five minutes to go get Jade, when it should have taken fifteen. The third red flag was when Jade slammed a tree without running track on a well-groomed walking trail that was almost too easy to do. The fourth red flag was his brother calling him just a few minutes later after Jade treed the coon to see what happened.

After thinking of how the night went, I felt like I should have stuck up for myself a little more and said no to buying Jade. It is still my belief that after the second drop, the owner of Jade wanted to go get Jade alone so he had time to call his brother and have him release a coon up a tree at a planned location that was easy to get to. It would be a piece of cake for Jade to tree with no track to run but a real hot coon still in the tree. That would explain why it took so long for him to come back and, not to mention the slow drive to the third (staged) location. It gave time to get the coon there and ready by his brother. I also wonder if his brother was still in the woods when we got to the tree or if he was at home. Maybe when we got back to the truck and headed back, did his brother really ask if it worked or if we bought it, instead of if Jade treed a coon. I guess we will never know, but one thing is for sure; I was pretty sure that we just bought ourselves a real expensive pot licker.

We got back home and went hunting for about two weeks with Jade and never saw a coon. We went hunting with a good friend of mine and he went just to see Jade go. After seeing what Jade did, he was also convinced that she was running the track backwards. After my brother was told by our friend that she was backtracking, he too, was convinced that she was no good. I wanted to prove it to myself that I could tell what a dog was doing on track. I trapped a coon and headed to the woods with Jade. I left Jade in the dog box and dragged the coon in a cage through the woods, across a road and then let the coon go free. I then led Jade in a half circle to the place I last saw the coon. I unhooked Jade and sure enough, she ran the track all the way back to the truck. Then she treed on the tailgate. To say the least, I was sure sick to my stomach. My brother at the time also had a neighbor that had a coon getting in the grain bin in his horse barn. We saw the coon run across the road, through the creek and up in the pasture. So I went and got Jade, the only dog we had at the time. She ran the track all the way back to the barn and treed on the door of the grain bin. Although Jade was a big disappointment, my brother and I got a real education on buying dogs and what to look out for when buying a dog.

My advice is if you see any red flags when you are interested in buying a dog, listen to your instincts that are telling you something is wrong, no matter how far you have to travel because, actually, that is all the more reason to make sure the dog is that much more of a real-deal coondog. But also remember that dogs are not perfect. People are not perfect either, none of us are. So no matter what kind of coondog trick someone wants to pull on you, God almighty wants us to forgive them just like our Lord Jesus taught us to do. Keep the Holy Spirit in your heart at all times even in a night hunt. So if the coon isn't there, then speak up and say it isn't there. Don't just go with the worldly flow. My brother had competed in a night hunt at a local club and I was back up handler when the cell phone trick was used against us and it didn't work that time.

CHAPTER 10

Home Remedies

There are some home remedies that I use on my own hounds that I have come up with. First, I would like to say I am not a veterinarian, so try these at your own risk. The following are just old time cheap remedies that I have found that work very well for me.

Ear Mites

If you don't know if your dog has ear mites or not, first look in your dog's ear. If you see that your hound has a dirty brown substance in the ear, this is the home of the ear mite. The naked eye can't see ear mites, but the brown feces is one sure way of knowing you need to treat your dog for them. Also, the dog's ear will have a bad smell to it from the ear mites. Finally, if you notice that your hound shakes its head while barking or right after it barks, then you should treat it for ear mites. What I do is I like to use two large water bottles, somewhere around a sixteen-ounce bottle in our case. The first bottle I fill up with lukewarm water. Then the second bottle I fill up also, but I put a squirt of liquid dish soap in the bottom of the bottle before the water goes in. Put just a little more than what would cover the bottom; it should be really soapy. Shake it up really good. Now, I also grab a handful of Q-tips. I put my dog on a leash and lay the dog's head up against my leg. Gently fold or lay the hound's ear back over its head and carefully clean the dog's ear out with the Q-tip. Once you have done that, take the pure lukewarm water and rinse out the dog's ear completely. Rub the dog's ear with his ear folded back on his own head. After that, take the bottle with the soap and water and pour it in the dog's ear, with it folded down. Rub the dog's ear. Do the method on both ears until the water is gone, and use plain water to finish rinsing out the dog's ear. I usually do this for a week straight once or twice a day and the ear mites are gone. Some dogs love this done to them and others just seem to tolerate it. But in all, the dogs are healthier and act much better when the week is over. They also shouldn't shake their head while barking or after barking. The brown substance should be gone. The dog's ear shouldn't stink anymore and you should see the true color of the inside of the ear again.

Peroxide is another solution that I have had good success with. I simply clean out the dog's ears with four or five Q-tips at once, per ear. Then, I pour peroxide in the hound's ear and fold the ear back over and rub each ear for about 10 seconds. This also takes a few days. Whether I use the soap or the peroxide, I always flush both ears out and rinse them with clear lukewarm water. I don't use these methods for more than seven days straight and I usually only treat the dogs once a day. I have had dogs given to me that professional veterinarian medicine would not cure the ear mite problems that the dogs would have. After a lot of money on expensive medications I was frustrated and started thinking outside of the box on my own and came up with these solutions that work and are inexpensive. These products are not in any way harmful to the dog. Most of the dogs come to start enjoying the procedure. I found most of the hounds would lay into my leg in great pleasure, almost as if they were getting their belly scratched.

Visine

I had a dog that had an irritation of the eyes. Both eyes were runny with clear liquid and matter. It was clear to me that the dog was allergic to something and it was probably in his bedding. I wiped his eyes out with a washcloth, rinsed them with lukewarm water and then squirted some Visine in them. I did this once a day for three days and what a difference! The dog's eyes cleared up and I never had that problem with him again. I also changed his bedding. I recommend using straw for bedding and not hay. This is for two reasons. One, the hay holds moisture in and the wet damp hay will also freeze in the wintertime. The other reason is because straw tends to have less weeds and other material that some dogs can be sensitive towards.

Aspirin

Aspirin is used for all sorts of things for humans and I learned that it can be beneficial to a dog as well. I used to be employed at a professional dog kennel that was nationally known for its English Bird dogs. One day my boss, who was also the owner, said to me, "Bill, give that old dog two crushed up aspirin and hide it in his canned dog food." So I did. Now this dog had arthritis so bad, it was hard for him to walk or get up. But after two hours, he was outside in the fenced-in lawn running at full speed with the other dogs. Now don't get me wrong, it is not the fountain of youth or anything, but it can help a poor old dog that isn't far from the happy hunting grounds.

CHAPTER 11

The Mighty Blue Hound

Late November brought on a dusting of snow. The coon had not been moving good as of late. The coon that were out, their tracks seemed to go from the den trees down to the creek and right back up the snowy banks of the creeks to their very place of refuge. The hunter knew any hot-nosed poodle could figure out those early tracks. But he wanted to test the very nose power and stick-to-it that the hard track would require to finish out from point A to point B and not get hung up in between. This hunter had a black and white hound, a red dog, a black and tan hound, a brindle dog, a redtick hound, a merle colored dog and a bluetick hound.

The hunter knew of a real big male coon that was in his prime of life and would test the very best of the hunter's cooners. He had been treed by the hunter when he was a much younger coon. He was easy to spot due to the coon having no tail from birth. So if he knew that and if the pack of hounds did tree him, the bobbed tailed coon would be the proof of the difficulty of the very track.

Bobbed Tail was a loner that lived on the very tip of the north end of the five-mile swamp. A decision made by Bobbed Tail early in his life, due to the over hunting of the south end of the swamp. The hunter set off about an hour before dark to seek the tracks of the bobbed tail coon, who was only known by the hunter with the, for now, multi colored pack of hounds.

He arrived in the area where he had spotted the coon before. Checking the icy culvert, sure enough, he had found the tracks of a mature coon and where the coon had sat eating off of a dead deer carcass. There were no tail tracks in the freshly powdered dusting of snow. The hunter thought that if it wasn't Bobbed Tail, it was still a real big coon judging by the size of the tracks. The hunter went back home, grabbed a cheeseburger from the wood stove that his wife had made him, along with a thermos full of ice water and headed out to load up the dogs. All of his hounds were good coondogs. No dog is perfect and not all dogs can finish every track they start, but if one of these dogs could tree this old coon, then the hunter just might think about a concentrated breeding of the bloodline, and get down to only one breed.

He unhooked the dogs all at once and off they went. Figuring this track to be about an hour and a half old, he didn't know if any would strike early or not. Then about two minutes into the ordeal, the blue hound gave tongue with a thunderous bawl that would rock the very foundation of his being. The hunter followed close and observed every hound in the pack. The blue hound out front and putting distance in between every strike of his voice, he, at this point, was separating himself from the rest of the pack, due to his nose power and cold trailing abilities.

The other hounds had their noses to the ground trying to pick up the scent, but just couldn't.

The hunter followed the pack as the blue dog pressed on and moved the track with authority as to say to the coon with his huge mouth, "Watch out coon 'cause I'm coming to getcha!" The trail led over blow-downs of snow covered hemlocks, ice covered bogs, up steep ravines and back into the deepest, darkest parts of the inner swamp and it's decaying inner workings. Perfect conditions for coon and hard on man and dog alike. About a half hour into the hunt, the black and tan dog opened, and about ten seconds later the red dog struck. A minute later the redtick, brindle, merle and black and white dog chimed in. At this point the rest of the pack was catching up to the blue hound, but he was still the chief dog at that point. Then they reached the part of the swamp that the hunter had nick-named the "plains area." This was an area that was flat and filled with stubbles and dead goldenrod, waist high. An area where coon and hound could really make distance fast! It was at this time when the hunter noticed that the black and white hound separated himself from the rest of the pack and take the lead. He did so because he was able to pick his head up with his nose in the air and drift the track. The blue dog was close behind with his head about a foot off the ground and moving fast. The rest of the pack was doing well and working hard. They kept their noses to the ground. When they reached the other side of the plains, the black and white dog and the blue hound made it about one hundred yards into the thick, snow covered tundra of the five-mile hemlock swamp. The black and white dog let out a locate and quickly settled into a hard, steady ringing chop on the tree.

The blue dog was with him, but wasn't treeing. The blue dog had circled the tree to make sure that the coon didn't climb and jump, but sure enough, that's just what the bobbed tail coon had done. He had climbed about twenty feet in the air, up the tree and walked out on a limb that reached over to a nearby bank and kept running. At that point, the blue hound picked up the track on top of the bank and pushed it with a flat out drive of determination to catch the bobbed tail coon.

Two minutes later the black and tan hound and the red dog made it to the tree and the black and white dog stayed, thinking he had the coon up the right tree. Then a minute later the rest of the pack showed up and stayed with the black and white dog. The red dog and the black and tan dog checked and picked up the track on top of the bank where the blue dog had a few minutes earlier. It was about five minutes after that, that the bluetick let out a locate that could be heard for miles. It rolled over into a steady loud dying bawl. About two and a half minutes later the black and tan and the red hounds had made it to the blue dog's tree as well. Sure enough, when the hunter showed up it was Bobbed Tail that sat high in a huge bare maple. Wow, he thought, what a hard cold track that was. He gathered up his hounds and went home.

Sitting there in his rocking chair in front of the Fisher wood stove he started evaluating the night's events and how everything unfolded. The redtick, the brindle plot, the leopard hound and treeing walker did good but came up short in the end. The bluetick, black and tan, and the redbone all found the right tree, but the bluetick tried it first. So he decided to sell all of his dogs except the bluetick and started a bluetick kennel and Chief was the foundation stock. As for Bobbed Tail, the hunter knew he would stay living in the swamp. So he never killed the coon. He figured that if a dog could tree that coon in that swamp, then the dog could tree a coon anywhere! The hunter thought to himself that Wyatt Earp was right when he said, "Speed is nice, but accuracy is everything." The Mighty Blue Hound.

CHAPTER 12

Family and Little Ones

This chapter is dear to my heart because I have a wife and 4 children. My family is involved in everything that I do and coon doggin' is no different. My family goes to church with me, helps me with the family business and goes to the woods with me as well. My daddy was disabled to the point of being crippled, but he always found the strength and heart to take his two boys to the woods for fishing, deer, turkey and coonhunting until he got too disabled.

It must be understood that the future of our sport and other hunting adventures are all in the responsibility of the elder generations to make sure that our youth in America at least get the chance to be introduced to God and his wonderful creation that we call the Great Outdoors and what it has to offer.

Sometimes it is challenging and stressful to take the little ones to field trials, bench shows, water races and when they are older, to night hunts, but we owe it to them, ourselves and the ones who came before us to do our part in helping them find an outlet to peer pressure from things like drugs, alcohol, sex, violence and anything else that would deter them from what the good Lord intended them to do, which is to have a relationship with our Lord.

There is nothing like taking a youngster to the woods and letting them hear the hounds open up for the first time. Also, for the first time they realize why the hound is barking. The thrill of the chase for the little ones is what it is all about. When it is cool, dark, and the stars are shining above, you're all geared up with your light and .22, the night time creatures are out, the farmers' field smells of cow manure and Old Duke lets out a ten second bawl. Let me tell you, if coonhunting is in your blood, those ingredients just mentioned will make the butterflies wiggle in your stomach. We need only to think back when we first felt like we got bit by the bug of coonhunting to see what we would like to help the kids experience down into their generation. If it takes letting them go out with a different breed than you like to hunt, then so be it. Let's not be so strict as to drive them away from something so beneficial to the heart and mind. I have hunted, owned and liked Bluticks, Redbones, Walkers, Plotts, Black and Tans, English, mixed breeds, and Majestics I would only advise you to pick the right bloodline in whatever breed the child prefers to try with the right traits that they would like and you will both be happy. I have been happy and disappointed with all breeds and it boils down to the right ingredients. I have not tried a Leopard hound yet, but I want to in the future. There are dogs that are good pup trainers and I think there are dogs that are good kid trainers as well. What I mean by that is, I would not advise any one to take a youngster or even someone who is older to the woods with a dog who will knock the back of the woods out. Let's understand that they are new to this game and it should be made easy and fun to them and not hard or miserable. Watch the weather forecast and pick a night that is clear and good tracking conditions. Also, if you could use a hot-nosed dog, the chase will be shorter and the action will be exciting. When the corn is in the milk and the hound is an open trailer, you have great coonhunting conditions.

So take a good kid trainer to the corn and let the memories begin. Remember, we all will be old someday and what a joy it will be to be blessed to sit down with that youngster someday when they are no longer youngsters and hear them tell you about the first time that they remember when you took them coonhunting.

One thing I remember doing when I was a little one is going to a place way back of the farm and building a camp fire in the middle of the road that split the two hayfields. We would cook marshmallows or hot dogs, drink coffee and listen to the dogs run track. This also allowed us to mix in some family time with the coonhunt.

Last summer my wife and I took the kids camping and I brought my coondogs along with us so I could hunt at night. My cousins went with me while my wife and mother-in-law sat at the campfire socializing. On one of the days I was sure glad I brought the hounds. While my wife was cooking chicken on the fire, a coyote came down the bank and my hounds let the world know they didn't want him around. It made what could have been a close call into a safer situation. Also, last summer my Treeing Walker female became a bench show champion and afterwards all the kids got to show the dog. They all received trophies for participation. I have let my son, as well as my niece, enter my dog, Amber, and they both went home with trophies and smiles from my dog. I think the younger you get your family involved with coon hounds, the more likely they will stick with it for years to come. Also, keep an open mind about whatever aspect of the coondog world that they are interested in. If they don't care about competing in any event, but love to pleasure hunt, then encourage them, love, care and help them in any way that you can as long as it's not wrong in God's eyes. Remember that children are a blessing from God and we need to help them from homework to coonhunting and everything in between. It is important not to push them into it, though. Remember, just like puppies, kids need time to develop interest in the sport and not be pressured to act like they have to.

CHAPTER 13

The Lake

Up on the ridge on the east side of the valley lies what all of the locals call Smyrna Lake. When Tom was a boy it was privately owned and only Tom's family and one other family were allowed to fish the lake. Tom's mom and dad, D and Mae, were friends of the owners and that's how they had access to the lake. The family would live in the camper in the summertime at the lake. D's parents, Grandma and Grandpa, would also be there, too.

A typical day at the lake went something like this: Tom and Harry would get up and go down to the lake and wash the sleep from their eyes, as they listened to the Canadian Geese honking through the mist on the island that was on the west end of the lake. On their way back up the trail to camp they would gather the dried up hemlock twigs to start the campfire that had burnt out the night before. They only got the twigs closest to the tree trunks because they were the driest from the nights rain and heavy dew. After a short trip to the outhouse the boys would start the fire using the hemlock twigs and dry ash and maple wood they had split into small pieces with D's axe. When the fire was crackling and the flames were down to an even steady pace, Mae would put the grate over the open fire and get the pancakes ready for breakfast. Mae had the boys put the cement blocks around the fire so they were even and she could cook for years on them. Mae mixed up the pancake batter and got the bacon out of the ice chest. Next, she would put water and coffee grounds in a sauce pan and let them boil until it was good and black. She would then take it off the fire and let it settle. For after that it was Tom's job to strain the coffee using a clean dishcloth. Mae would cook brown eggs from our chickens, bacon from last winter's hog and pancakes.

They used homemade maple syrup and butter that Mae and Grandma made from the milking cow. When it was all ready Tom, Harry, D, Mae, Grandpa and Grandma would all sit at the picnic table and thank God for the blessings on and around the table. Then they would all dig in.

Once the dishes were done Mae would go for a horseback ride and D, Tom, Harry and Grandpa would go fishing in the boat. Grandma would sit in the car reading her western novels and waiting for the men to get back for lunch. One day, it was real hot and the fish were not biting real good. Tom knew that the fish always bit on a worm better than a lure, but the lake seemed dead and he needed some action! D, Grandpa and Harry all chewed tobacco and even their chew spit wasn't getting the bass to bite. Tom looked around and noticed a log in the water that he hadn't noticed before while they were fishing on the south side of the lake. It was within casting range so he thought, maybe the fish would be guarding a nest of eggs there. Tom got a Hoolapopper out of the tackle box, put it on the pole and threw it towards the log. Almost the very second it hit the water a large Bass lunged out of the water with its mouth wide and slammed the lure! "Oh my goodness, get the net, get the net!!" said Tom. What a fight it was! Up and down, left and right, jerking here and there, the pole bending to its limit. Tom finally got the fish to the edge of the boat, Harry got the net under the Bass and the hook came out! Splash right into the net! "Holy Cow" Grandpa said, "Look at the size of that fish!" What a dandy it was too. It was a five-pound large mouth Bass at 19 inches. What a whopper for Tom; it was the biggest Bass he had ever caught. Later that night it would be revealed by Tom, when dressing out the fish, that there was a six-inch Bullhead in the belly of the Bass. So Tom figured that the Bass had been guarding a nest, because it sure wasn't hungry!

The two boys got to not like the taste of fish and from then on would practice catch and release or put the fish in a trap for a coon that needed catching. Of course, if there wasn't anything else to eat, a little salt would work on them to make them taste better. Everyone got back to shore and Mae showed up with her horse. Grandma brought out the liverwurst sandwiches and lemonade in the big cooler from the trunk of the car and put them on the picnic table. Those were good times for Tom when he was growing up. Just doesn't seem right that the world would be eventually taken away by time, money, death and politics. Not to mention the rich hands of the city folks that would purchase the lake and land and only view the property as a profit.

The Mohawk and Cherokee blood that runs in Tom's veins cry out to those who bought the lake, "I was here first and when will you go away? You came here like a bandit coon in the cornfield at night to rob me of my harvest and now I am left here hungry, alone, scared and feeling as if my world has been stripped of all the blessings that God has given to me!" Times-r-a-changin'.

CHAPTER 14

Times R A Changin'

Back when Tom was a young lad, things were different. When I say different, I mean things like, no cell phones, no laptops, kids didn't get homework until the third grade, you could tell a boy from a girl because boys and girls dressed different. Boys didn't get earrings and girls had long hair unless they had medical problems. Yes, sir, the face of Tom's world back when he grew up, it all was a lot simpler. Why even in the coondog world, (a sport Tom truly loves to this day) things have changed. There were no GPS units or shock collars. There used to be farms around that Tom would hunt on near his house and now they are all gone; sold to the highest bidder from far away cities. Cabins were built on the land and cameras are all around to alert the new owners, day or night. Tom grew up in a place called Smyrna Valley. Things in the Valley just didn't change much at all. When people think of New York the first thing that comes to one's mind is New York City. But the outsiders don't know that upstate New York is as country as you can get, especially in Smyrna Valley. In the Valley, all the families are related through Tom's mother's side. So old fashion runs deep in Tom's veins. There are four different families in the Valley, all from the same blood, on one side.

Coondogs, chickens and horses were the big to-do in young Tom's life. He also raised beef cows with his twin brother Harry. The two boys' parents were very poor, so in order to buy school clothes they raised Holstein-Herford cross stock all fall, winter and spring. Then they sold them to the cattle dealer in the spring for cash money for school clothes and supplies. They also worked like dogs in the summer in the hayfields putting in hay for ten farms around. They were also able to gain access to hunt coon with their hounds on the farms to help keep the coon out of the cornfields.

One hot summer day, Tom and Harry had been throwing hay bales all day long. They had talked about going coonhunting later on that night, in between wagon changes. After the boys got done they headed to the house and relaxed on the porch swing. Grandma brought out some homemade switchel and double-layered German chocolate cake. Oh yeah, good times. Tom, Harry, Grandma and Grandpa sat there relaxed and talked about coondogs and enjoyed the cool breeze that would briefly cut the hot heat of the sun. The dark spell came (or nighttime, as most folks call it) and the boys grabbed their light, compasses and dogs. They threw them in their dad's old Ford and waited for him to take them hunting. "Boys, go kiss your mother," Dad would say, because in those days, you kissed your mom and dad before you left. It was impolite if you didn't. Times are a changing for the worse in these days, thought Tom.

After the boys kissed Mom, they headed for the woods. Dad always had a bag of apples and a Thermos full of coffee to take to the woods and always a roll of toilet paper in the glove box, just in case. It was a cool summer night. Black sky and white stars with no breeze. The bluetick's name was Suzie. She knew no quit and in those days neither did the boys, Tom and Harry. Suzie started the track in the bottom of a Hemlock swamp. A deep dark place on earth indeed! Working her way through the low laying boughs and water, the ringtail used his craft to try to evade the top cooner, but to no avail. Suzie bawled here and there, putting distance in between every bawl. Through the water and over the maple logs she did prove a hearty champion. The boys' dad's name was D, a simple man just like his name. D, yup, that's right, just plain D! He was a wartime vet and didn't boast much about anything, even cooning. D just let the dog do the talking. The three stopped to listen to old Suzie. She went quiet. Then all at once she let out a huge long bawl and rolled it over to a steady chop. D told the boys, "Sounds like she's treed to me, boys!" So they went to her. Tom crossed the creek and Harry followed. D hooked her up and after a few minutes, they spotted the coon looking down on them with two amber eyes. "Good girl Suzie," D told her as he loved her up at the bottom of the tree and the boys followed suit. With their lights blazing and Dad using the compass, they made their way out of the swamp to the dirt road.

It seemed like a long time to wait to use the lights the boys had got for Christmas, but after that first hunt it was all worth it. You see, in those days, hunters didn't shoot coon out of season. They left that old crafty ringtail to make more tracks next time. D always told the boys that if you have to shoot every coon that your dog trees to keep your dog wanting to tree coon, then you are shooting the wrong animal. Yeah, times are a changing.

While growing up the two hillbilly boys by the age of twelve could shoot bow, fish, cut firewood, ride horse, hunt coon, deer, turkey, coyote and trap anything that needed to be caught. Tom woke up to the rooster crowing and knew what needed to be done that day. The horse stalls needed to be cleaned. The boys hated that because for some reason they couldn't clean them every day. So when it was time to clean them, the horse manure was three feet deep. Each stall was a ten by ten box stall. This was work that a lot of grown men today wouldn't even think of tackling. They could use a skid steer. Tom and Harry's parents were poor so that was out of the question. Tom was taller but Harry was stronger. They gave it their all year after year. The boys got up and the sun hit them right in the face. Hot and hazy, they would quit only for a glass of spring water and then back at it. Lunchtime rolled around and Mom made them meat pie; hamburg and peas. The boys would talk about coonhunting at lunch and couldn't wait to get the barn cleaned. Each stall had a spreader load of manure in it, but they used the old Ford pickup because they couldn't afford a spreader. They forked it on, drove it to the hayfield or pasture and one of the boys would commence to forking it off while the other one would drive slow.

All burnt and blistered, the boys ate supper. Suppertime meant more hamburg but with gravy and white bread, a glass of water and a cup of coffee. It felt good to rest their backs for a spell. The air on the porch of the cabin became cool as Tom sat by himself. He had time to think about God, his family, school and what he might be when he grew up. He knew that Harry and himself already outworked a lot of men and being only twelve, was that the path that they should take, he wondered?

Tom had loved God ever since he could remember. He would come closer to God every day; at least he would hope he sure could. Then the screen door to the cabin opened and his dad stepped out and said, "You want to hunt tonight Tom?" "Yee haw!" Tom said and with that, it was off to another adventure to the woods.

CHAPTER 15

The Right Track

As time went on in Tom's life, he was in his early twenties and he had worked hard and hunted hard. He also played sports the same way. But there was still something missing in his life. He believed in our Lord, Jesus and had a sanitation business that he co-owned with his brother Harry, but still Tom was lonely in a way that nothing could fix in a young man's heart, except the touch and companionship of a woman. Tom thought about this and knew after a lot of thought that only a woman that knew the Lord and understood Tom's ways and how much he loved coonhunting would do! You see, most of society wouldn't understand that Tom loved a sport that most people do not understand. He loved God and that was genuine. He grew up hard and out of touch and was sheltered in most peoples' standards.

This might have been true, but he had a heart of gold. One would witness that if someone was in pain and if Tom were around, he would help them no matter their color or race. Why? Because Tom knew we are all God's children.

Tom spoke with his mom and dad about it and they thought the same about the girls in town. They would only see the hillbilly in Tom and judge him on that basis alone, not his heart and mind. Also, his willingness to provide for his family the way God intended it. His mom and dad reminded Tom of the Indian girl, Kate, that lived up the road on the hill in the Valley. She and her mother had moved to the area from Virginia when she was just a baby. Kate and Tom were only a few years apart in age and in fact, she was the one who had been Tom's friend and partner when they were growing up coonhunting, playing softball, basketball and cards. She also was the one who had visited Tom and his family at the lake when growing up.

"Wow," Tom said to his parents, "I wonder what she thinks of me?" "Go and ask her," they said. It took Tom a few days of thinking to muster up the nerve. After all, he liked her a lot and she was beautiful. She believed and did the same things Tom did but what if she doesn't think of me like that? he thought. Man I must have been so busy coonhunting, deerhunting and paying so much attention to my hounds that I didn't ever notice that Kate and I got along better than two peas in a pod! "Oh boy," Tom was so excited that he couldn't sleep well that night. He thought to himself that he should ask Kate to go coonhunting with him tomorrow night and just see how she acts around Tom and what type of response she gives Tom.

The next night came and just before dark Tom rode his horse up to the old barn where Kate was collecting chicken eggs for her mother. Tom hitched his horse to the hitching post in front of the barn and Kate came out to greet him. She herself had great joy and butterflies in her stomach whenever she saw Tom. He said, "Want to go hunting tonight?" She responded and said, "We can if you want to but, I was thinking it would be fun to ride double on your horse, if we could go on a trail ride and talk later," A real big smile came across Tom's face as he quickly processed the seemingly enchanting words coming from the doey-eyed Kate. "Why of course we could, I would like that very much," said Tom. Kate responded, "I will bring the eggs to Mom and then we could go." Kate walked the eggs in the wire basket up the road to her mother's. Her mother liked Tom and knew that it would be alright for the two to go riding together. As soon as the two were on the horse and riding off, from that point on it was clear that true love was in the air.

They rode up on the ridge that Tom knew well; it was where he had hunted deer and coon for years. They talked about love, life and most importantly God. Tom explained to Kate that above all else that the most important thing in Tom's life was God, Jesus his Lord and Savior, and the Holy Spirit. Tom told Kate that he was looking for his very own wife to love forever. But that he needed to find someone with the same faith. She understood and rode on for a while. Just before dark they stopped the horse for a break.

Tom thought to himself, it's now or never. With butterflies in both of their stomachs, their eyes met and their hands held one another, totally focused on each other's every movement, Tom said, "You know Kate, I like you more than just a friend." Kate said "I think I do too, but I have to think about it." Tom said, "I understand." And he brought her back home.

The following night they went coonhunting. They sat under the clear starry night waiting for the dogs to strike. Kate spoke first and said, "My grandmother used to take me to church when she would come up to visit from Virginia. She believed in God and so do I." She told Tom. "And I think you know that I like you more than a friend, too, Tom." This put a smile on Tom's face from ear to ear.

This would prove to be the right move for both of them as they would later get married and have children of their own, whom they would raise to know, worship and love the Lord! They would teach them that hunting, fishing, family and even work were from the Lord and they are all for the right reasons.

Testimonies

I am writing this chapter because we are supposed to share our testimony with others. I do hope and pray that this might plant a seed in the reader for the Lord and maybe shed some light on why I believe in what I believe in, which is God. I am out spoken about the Lord, but very humble and also shy about worldly conversations. This is all because of one event that changed my life forever!

My brother and I were running our sanitation business that we had started out of high school and doing a lot of physical labor. I was also on a diet of no sodium or salt. This was to try to make sure that I didn't end up overweight. One day, we were working hard and all at once I felt light headed, dizzy and short of breath. I looked at the ground and then at the sky. I looked at our truck and then at my brother. I then said, "Lytle, I don't feel good." He said, "Oh, just go sit in the truck and you will get feeling better." Then I took about three or four steps towards the truck and fell to the ground in a spinning motion that left me lying flat on my back and on the sidewalk looking at the sky. I said, "I can't breathe." At this point my brother was shaking me and telling me, "Wake up Bill, wake up." I was going in and out of consciousness and I said to my brother, "Go get help." He ran to the door of the customer that we were picking up and dialed 911. When I came to, my customer was holding my head in his arms telling me something I will never forget. He said, "Jesus loves you, you will be okay! Jesus loves you, you will be okay!"

I then took in my last breath that I could feel and felt my heart beat for the last time. I can only tell you that this is the most helpless and awful feeling that I think you can experience outside of losing a child. There was a small pause in time and then I felt this warm peaceful, nice, soothing, relaxing, awesome feeling. I had felt nothing like it before or since. I really can't do it justice in human words. I then saw this bright, white light. Not like a lamp, but all of the air in front of me and all around me was overwhelming full of this bright light. Then I felt this warm humble feeling. I have never felt so peaceful in my whole life. In fact, I didn't want to leave at that point. I then called out, "God is that you? God is that you?" Then I thought, maybe I should ask if it was Jesus. So I said, "Jesus is that you?" Now I wonder if I should have asked if it were the Holy Spirit. At this point all I could think about were the people who I loved the most in my life at the time which was my dad, mom, brother and my former girlfriend. I then, all of a sudden, started feeling really bad, almost awful. Instantly, I was breathing again and looking at the sky. The EMT's were putting on the air mask and strapping me down. There were wires and hoses hooked to me like a car engine. I was in the ambulance being monitored. The one man said, "I have a pulse," and the other one said, "Yeah, but look at the straight line on the monitor screen," It then started showing a heartbeat. I was crying and in shock to say the least! The EMT said, "Son, are you under a lot of stress?" I said, "Yes," and started crying harder. They then looked at each other and instantly the one man said, "Yeah, he's on something for sure."

Now I have never done drugs! EVER! And I never will! I don't drink, smoke or anything except work too hard sometimes. I finally went to a cardiologist who discovered that my blood stream did not have enough salt in it to properly regulate the electrical part of my heart. I was only 21 years old and had gotten a second chance in life. Dear reader, I ask you: DO YOU BELIEVE IN GOD? I DO 100%!!

Since then I have had a stomach surgery at the age of 29 and two heart surgeries at the age of thirty-one. This is risky enough but I am also allergic to anesthesia. It is a condition called malignant hyperthermia. This adds a whole new level of fear, but with faith and a good anesthesiologist it is now much less risky.

My second testimony has to do with hard times and hard lessons. My brother and I were in the trash business for 9 years and then decided to sell our business and buy another one in the Adirondack Mountains. It was a motel on the lake. Sounded great compared to a trash business, but again I thought I should do what God wanted. So I prayed and said to God that no matter how this turns out, if it is the path that you want me to take, then my faith is in your hands and I will follow where you lead me. I talked this over with my brother, Lytle, and his wife, Casey, my mom and my wife and we all agreed to go, except Mom would travel the two hours back and forth. My wife also didn't really like the idea because of the distance away from her family. But she loved me and wanted to be there for the family and me. As time went on we all felt it on our hearts that Sunday was not when God wanted us to work. So we changed the rules to live more like God wanted us to even if we lost business over it. Nobody is perfect and we all had our good points and bad points. In the end, the economy was the reason we eventually had to get out of the motel business. But as the Lord works in mysterious ways, there was another garbage business that was for sale and it was looking really good to our families to get back into something we knew more about. This brought on more hardships as we spent almost every last bit of money we had trying to keep the motel afloat.

I prayed to God a lot because this trash business was not really big enough to support both families and I went to apply for a job at the State Highway Department. I had to get hired or lose my car and house and not be able to feed my family. One day the State called and set me up for a physical. The next day the garbage business had a chance to get three times bigger. I was faced with the choice to take the State rate and benefits and leave my brother and his family hanging or take another leap of faith, put my trust in God and pray that he would pull us through and come out on top again. This time Lytle, Casey, Mom and I put everything we had into it and with the help of my wife and God, we pulled it off. My wife is now a stay at home Mom, but she also threw trash, as well as Lytle's wife, to help get us going again. Casey is now in the office full time. Without my mom, neither families, my brother's nor mine, would not have what we have today.

To put it in prospective, as to how poor we were at that time, my wife and I, with our 9-month-old son, lived in our bedroom with a blanket for a door and an electric heater for our only heat source. It was 70 degrees in that room and the rest of the house was 30 degrees. We had to choose to pay the car payment or the house and I said they are not taking the house!

So that's what we paid. But we managed to be able to keep the car, thank God! I also kept my hounds alive by saving bread and scraps out of the dumpsters that we had on our trash route. Those were tough times, indeed! But it didn't last, as God has blessed us with a very good trash business and now supports two families with 11 people total and four other employees. Thank God for Mom, she still helps out. God brought us to these things and God has gotten us through them. Readers, put your faith in the Lord and you will never be sorry. God does love you! Jesus is our Savior from sin! The Holy Spirit guides you! It is the Holy Spirit that tells you, "Hey that is bad for you." Ask and pray to God on all that matters, he likes to hear from you. If you do your part, he will certainly do his.

About the Author

William lives in Central New York with his wife, Sarah, and their four children. He loves to hunt, fish, camp and most importantly, worship God. He is a member of the First Baptist Tabernacle Church. He owns and operates, along with his brother, Lytle, a sanitation business called ADK Disposal. William's mission is to be a disciple to other people by sharing his testimonies and faith-based stories.